Let's Read About Pets

Guinea Pigs

by JoAnn Early Macken

Reading consultant: Susan Nations, M.Ed., author/literacy coach/consultant

WEEKLY WR READER
EARLY LEARNING LIBRARY

Please visit our web site at: www.earlyliteracy.cc
For a free color catalog describing Weekly Reader® Early Learning Library's
list of high-quality books, call 1-877-445-5824 (USA) or 1-800-387-3178 (Canada).
Weekly Reader® Early Learning Library's fax: (414) 336-0164.

Library of Congress Cataloging-in-Publication Data

Macken, JoAnn Early, 1953-
 Guinea pigs / by JoAnn Early Macken.
  p. cm. — (Let's read about pets)
 Summary: Simple text and pictures briefly describe the physical characteristics
and behavior of guinea pigs and how to care for them as pets.
 Includes bibliographical references and index.
 ISBN 0-8368-3798-3 (lib. bdg.)
 ISBN 0-8368-3845-9 (softcover)
 1. Guinea pigs as pets—Juvenile literature. [1. Guinea pigs. 2. Pets.] I. Title.
SF459.G9M23 2003
636.9'3592—dc21
                                                        2003045038

First published in 2004 by
Weekly Reader® Early Learning Library
330 West Olive Street, Suite 100
Milwaukee, WI 53212 USA

Editorial: JoAnn Early Macken
Art direction: Tammy Gruenewald
Page layout: Katherine A. Goedheer

Printed in the United States of America

1 2 3 4 5 6 7 8 9 07 06 05 04 03

Note to Educators and Parents

Reading is such an exciting adventure for young children! They are beginning to integrate their oral language skills with written language. To encourage children along the path to early literacy, books must be colorful, engaging, and interesting; they should invite the young reader to explore both the print and the pictures.

Let's Read About Pets is a new series designed to help children learn about the joys and responsibilities of keeping a pet. In each book, young readers will learn interesting facts about the featured animal and how to care for it.

Each book is specially designed to support the young reader in the reading process. The familiar topics are appealing to young children and invite them to read — and re-read — again and again. The full-color photographs and enhanced text further support the student during the reading process.

In addition to serving as wonderful picture books in schools, libraries, homes, and other places where children learn to love reading, these books are specifically intended to be read within an instructional guided reading group. This small group setting allows beginning readers to work with a fluent adult model as they make meaning from the text. After children develop fluency with the text and content, the book can be read independently. Children and adults alike will find these books supportive, engaging, and fun!

— Susan Nations, M.Ed., author, literacy coach, and consultant in literacy development

Guinea pigs are born with teeth and fur. Their eyes are open when they are born. Baby guinea pigs are called **piglets**.

Guinea pigs may have short fur or long fur. Some have fur that is silky and shiny. Some have stripes or spots in their fur.

Some guinea pigs have rough **coats**. Their fur grows in patterns that look like circles.

Guinea pigs are **rodents** like mice, rats, and gerbils. Their teeth always keep growing.

Guinea pigs chew on things. If you let your pet loose, watch your tables and chairs! Can you guess why?

Guinea pigs can eat flakes or pellets of food. They like to eat carrots, apples and oranges. They also need fresh water.

A guinea pig can live in a hutch or a cage. Cover the bottom with wood shavings and hay.

17

Happy guinea pigs gurgle and jump. If you hear teeth clicking, be careful! An angry guinea pig might bite.

Guinea pigs need room to run. In nice weather, they like to go outside and eat grass. But watch them. They like to hide!

Glossary

hutch — a pen or cage for an animal

patterns — designs or forms

pellets — small pieces of food

rodents — small gnawing mammals such as mice or squirrels

For More Information

Fiction Books

Meade, Holly. *John Willy and Freddy McGee.*
  New York: Marshall Cavendish, 1998.
Shannon, Margaret. *Gullible's Troubles.*
  Boston: Houghton Mifflin, 1998.

Nonfiction Books

Buck, Gisela. *Gertie and Gus the Guinea Pigs.*
  Milwaukee: Gareth Stevens, 1997.
Hughes, Sarah. *My Guinea Pig.* New York:
  Children's Press, 2001.

Web Sites
Cavies (Guinea Pigs)
worldkids.net/critters/mischief/cavies.htm
How to handle, play with, and care for a guinea pig

Index

About the Author

JoAnn Early Macken is the author of two rhyming picture books, *Sing-Along Song* and *Cats on Judy*, and three other series of nonfiction books. She teaches children to write poetry, and her poems have appeared in several children's magazines. A graduate of the M.F.A. in Writing for Children and Young Adults program at Vermont College, she lives in Wisconsin with her husband and their two sons.